The Appalachians
and Other U.S. Mountain Ranges

Jennifer Prior, Ph.D.

Consultant

Brian Allman
Principal
Upshur County Schools, West Virginia

Publishing Credits

Rachelle Cracchiolo, M.S.Ed., *Publisher*
Emily R. Smith, M.A.Ed., *SVP of Content Development*
Véronique Bos, *VP of Creative*
Dona Herweck Rice, *Senior Content Manager*
Dani Neiley, *Editor*
Fabiola Sepulveda, *Series Graphic Designer*

Image Credits: p4 Library of Congress [LC-DIG-highsm-44398]; p7 (bottom)
Tennessee Valley Authority; p9 (top) Juan Melli/Take A Hike!; p32 Alamy/Christian
Kober 1; all other images from iStock and/or Shutterstock

Library of Congress Cataloging-in-Publication Data

Names: Prior, Jennifer Overend, 1963- author.
Title: The Appalachians and other U.S. mountain ranges / Jennifer Prior.
Description: Huntington Beach : Teacher Created Materials, 2022 | Includes
  index. | Audience: Grades 4-6 | Summary: "The United States is home to
  countless mountain ranges. They vary in size from small to very large.
  They are as different as east and west. In this book, you will learn
  about four major mountain ranges in the United States"-- Provided by
  publisher.
Identifiers: LCCN 2022021305 (print) | LCCN 2022021306 (ebook) | ISBN
  9781087691077 (paperback) | ISBN 9781087691237 (ebook)
Subjects: LCSH: Mountains--United States--Juvenile literature. | Mountain
  ecology--United States--Juvenile literature.
Classification: LCC GB525 .P75 2022 (print) | LCC GB525 (ebook) | DDC
  551.43/20973--dc23/eng/20220722
LC record available at https://lccn.loc.gov/2022021305
LC ebook record available at https://lccn.loc.gov/2022021306

Shown on the cover is the Blue Ridge Parkway
in the Appalachian Mountains.

5482 Argosy Avenue
Huntington Beach, CA 92649
www.tcmpub.com
ISBN 978-1-0876-9107-7

Table of Contents

Mountain Ranges in the United States

There are many mountain ranges in the United States. Some are small, while others are huge. Some mountain ranges are part of larger ones. No two mountain ranges are alike. Each has **unique** wildlife and plant life. Each has **distinct geological** features. And each has its own interesting landmarks.

Appalachians

Alaska Range

Sierra Nevada

The Appalachians are in the East. The Rocky Mountains are in the West. The Sierra Nevada is near the West Coast. And the Alaska Range is—you guessed it—in Alaska.

The Appalachian Mountains are covered with trees and have an **extensive** trail system. The Rocky Mountains have the world's second-longest mountain range. The Sierra Nevadas are home to some of the world's largest trees. And the Alaska Range has the highest peak in North America.

These mountains are just a glimpse of what the United States has to offer. Each is stunningly beautiful and attracts millions of tourists each year. It's all about fresh air, untouched nature, and incredible views. There's something truly amazing about the **vastness** of these great mountains.

Underwater Mountains

Did you know that some mountains are underwater? Most people think that Mount Everest is the highest mountain in the world. But Mauna Kea, a mountain that is mostly underwater, is about 33,500 feet (10,211 meters) high. That's about 4,471 feet (1,363 meters) taller than Mount Everest!

Appalachian Region

The Appalachian Mountains stretch nearly 2,000 miles (3,219 kilometers). They begin in northeastern Canada. They end in Alabama in the southern United States. The Appalachians are made up of many smaller mountain ranges. For example, the White Mountains are in New Hampshire. The Catskill Mountains are in New York. The Blue Ridge and Great Smoky Mountains are in the South.

The entire region is rich with water. It has many rivers, streams, springs, and waterfalls. It also has lakes. But there are not enough lakes to hold all the rain that falls. The southern part of the Appalachians receives roughly 70–90 inches (178–229 centimeters) of rain each year. Compare that to the Rocky Mountains. Most national forests in the Rockies receive about 20 or more inches (51 centimeters) of rain per year. In the past, heavy rainfall often led to flooding. Floodwaters are dangerous. They can cause great damage. So, a solution was needed. In 1933, the Tennessee Valley Authority (TVA) was formed. The TVA built a system of **dams**. These dams calm the dangerous waters. They create electric power. And they provide a number of lakes for people to enjoy.

Allegheny River

Apalachia Dam

Water Power

How does water create electricity? A dam holds water in a lake. When the water is released, it falls over the dam. Water falls with great force. It spins a **turbine**. The turbine **generates** electric power as it spins.

Footpath for the People

The Appalachian Trail is the longest hiking-only trail in the world. From Maine to Georgia, the trail offers hikers miles and miles of **scenic** wonder. Currently, there are about 2,190 miles (3,524 kilometers) of trail. But this can change as new paths are added. Hiking the entire trail is a huge task. It involves lots of training and preparation. Hikers who take on the challenge travel through 14 states! It takes an average of six months to complete. Hiking this distance is not for everyone. But hiking short stretches along the trail is popular with day hikers. Each year, three million people hike parts of the trail to see the amazing views.

100-Mile Wilderness

Family Finishes the Trail

The Crawford family from Kentucky successfully hiked the Appalachian Trail in 2018. The family of eight included six children, ages 2 to 16. The entire family finished the trail in five months.

Lemon Squeezer

Maine is famous for the 100-Mile Wilderness area. This 100-mile (161-kilometer) stretch is mostly **deserted** and offers breathtaking views.

The Lemon Squeezer in New York is a very narrow part of the trail. Hikers have to squeeze through rock formations.

Laurel Falls is an 80-foot (24-meter) waterfall in Tennessee. It gets its name from the flowering laurel shrub. It blooms along the trail in May.

Clingmans Dome is in the Great Smoky Mountains. At more than 6,500 feet (1,981 meters) in **elevation**, it is the highest point along the trail. On clear days, hikers can see over 100 miles (160 kilometers).

Clingmans Dome

Wildlife in the Wilderness

Imagine hiking in the Appalachians. You hear a sound. What is it? It is probably one of the many animals that live there. Since the Appalachians span from Canada to the southern United States, the **terrain** varies from place to place. And the animals living in each area are as varied as the terrain.

Black bears are the only bears found in these mountain ranges. They weigh up to 500 pounds (227 kilograms). That's about the same weight as a motorcycle or a piano! Hikers do not need to worry too much about black bears, though. They are mostly shy animals but will approach campsites if they smell food. So, storing food off the ground when camping is a must.

black bear

A huge animal in the northern Appalachians is the moose. Moose weigh almost three times more than black bears—1,400 pounds (635 kilograms)! They eat leaves and twigs and mostly stay away from people. Moose only tend to get aggressive if protecting their calves.

Many kinds of snakes live in the Appalachian Mountains. Some are **venomous**. Most are not. One venomous snake that is found primarily in the South is the pygmy rattlesnake. This spotted snake can grow to be about two and a half feet (0.76 meters) long. Its rattle, on the other hand, is so small, it can barely be heard.

pygmy rattlesnake

Did You Know?

In some places, moose are nicknamed rubber-nosed swamp donkeys. They have big noses and are good swimmers. Only the males have antlers. They use them to fight other moose during mating season. After mating season, the antlers drop off. They grow a new pair each year.

Boars are a kind of pig that live in the Appalachian Mountains, but they are not **native** to the area. They were brought over from Europe and escaped from hunting preserves. They bred with **domestic** pigs and now cause lots of problems. They use their noses to tear up the ground and eat everything from plants to nuts to small animals.

wild boar and piglet

Secret Weapon!

The wild boar carries its own secret weapon. It has tusks on its bottom lip. A male boar has longer tusks than a female. Unlike a female boar, a male also has tusks on his upper lip that are used for sharpening the lower ones.

While many birds live in these mountains, the ruffed grouse makes its home along the entire Appalachian Trail. This bird is the size of a chicken. Its color and markings help it stay **camouflaged** in the forests along the trail. Males make a drumming sound by flapping their wings. They also puff up black feathers around their necks, which form the "ruff."

Bobcats live, but are rarely seen, in the Appalachian Mountains. Their tan fur with brown spots helps them blend into their surroundings. Early settlers called bobcats "woods ghosts" because of their mysterious nature. A bobcat is about twice the size of a house cat. It has a short tail and long hairs that extend from the points of its ears. It makes its den in caves and hollow trees and hunts for small animals.

bobcat

ruffed grouse

Asheville, North Carolina

Life in the Mountains

The Appalachian Mountains are a great expanse of wilderness. But they are also home to many people. Numerous towns and cities are nestled into these mountains. Asheville, North Carolina, is one such town. It is tucked into the Blue Ridge Mountains. It is a popular tourist spot. Long ago, the land was home to the Cherokee Nation. But it was later settled by Europeans. In 1797, it became an outpost. Explorers stopped there for supplies. Davy Crockett and Daniel Boone were known to pass through.

Today, Asheville is known for its art. It is also known for its building design. Historic buildings have been well cared for. They give a feeling of the past. The downtown area draws people to modern art galleries. They also come for tasty food and live music. Though it is now quite modern, the city takes pride in sharing its history. The Asheville Urban Trail is a walking tour of the town's history. There's also the Museum of the Cherokee Indian. It tells the story of the tribe's 11,000 years of living in the area. Visitors can also learn about the history of African Americans. And they can learn about famous people who have ties to Asheville.

The Biltmore Estate is a historic house and museum in Asheville.

Apples, Apples, and More Apples!

One important industry that has been around for years in Appalachia is apple growing. Old family orchards that sell apples and cider can be found from Virginia down to Georgia.

Rocky Mountains

The world's second-longest mountain range can be found in the West. The Rocky Mountains are also known as "the Rockies." They run from northern Canada to New Mexico. They lack the water and greenery of the Appalachian Mountains. But they have higher peaks and magnificent views. Like the Appalachians, the Rockies have black bears. But they also have the larger and more dangerous grizzly bears. These mountains are home to many animals, but a symbol of the Rockies is the bighorn sheep. It is the largest sheep in North America. Most unique is how the sheep's hooves allow it to jump on rocks and climb up and down cliffs.

Trail Ridge Road is in Rocky Mountain National Park. Imagine what it would feel like to drive closer and closer up to a big, blue sky. That's why it is nicknamed "Highway to the Sky." One of the most popular sites along the road is the Continental Divide. This "Great Divide" is a tall ridge of mountains that separates the continent's water. Precipitation that falls on the west side of the Divide flows to the Pacific Ocean. Water and snow that fall on the east side flow to the Atlantic Ocean.

bighorn sheep

Tundra

If you keep driving up Trail Ridge Road, you will reach the tundra. That is an area that is so high up in elevation that very little grows. Extreme cold temperatures make it impossible for trees to grow.

Rocky Mountain Landmarks

There are countless impressive views in the Rocky Mountains. Many are accessible by paved roads or hiking trails. Forest Canyon Overlook is in Colorado. It offers a 360-degree view of the Rockies. This U-shaped canyon is at an elevation of 11,716 feet (3,571 meters). It was formed by a huge glacier. The glacier dug through the rock to form this amazing view of the tundra.

Quite possibly the most popular attraction in the Rocky Mountains is Old Faithful. It is in Yellowstone National Park. This is a **geyser** that pushes roughly 8,000 gallons (30,300 liters) of water high into the air. A geyser is a vent in Earth's surface. But do not get too close. It erupts with boiling water and steam. Old Faithful used to erupt about every hour. But now, the water spouts about every 90 minutes, although the time varies.

You can also hop in the car for an amazing Rocky Mountain drive in Montana. Going-to-the-Sun Road is in Glacier National Park. It is a narrow, two-lane road that passes towering mountains, waterfalls, and lakes. The road is so narrow that some vehicles are too wide to travel on it.

Going-to-the-Sun Road

Castle Geyser erupts in Yellowstone National Park.

Sierra Nevada

On the West Coast is the Sierra Nevada. Most of the range is in California. The eastern edge reaches into Nevada. It is home to the second-highest peak in the United States. Mount Whitney, in central California, is 14,494 feet (4,418 meters) above sea level. It is second only to Denali in Alaska.

Over time, mountain ranges change. **Erosion** causes them to break down from wind, ice, and water. This is true of the Sierra Nevadas. But the greatest source of change in these mountains is not from erosion. It is from human use of the land. Mining and logging have changed the landscape. But tourism has had a huge impact, too. The mountains are close to heavily populated areas. This makes them an ideal spot for recreational use. People **flock** to these mountains for hiking, fishing, and camping. They also come for off-roading, horseback riding, and snow sports.

The Sierra Nevada is home to some of the largest trees on the planet. Giant sequoias are found along the western slope of the mountain range. They can grow to be about 300 feet (91 meters) tall.

GENERAL SHERMAN

Towering Giants

What's so amazing about giant sequoias? Their branches can reach up to 8 feet (2.4 meters) in diameter. Their bark can grow up to 3 feet (1 meter) thick. And they can live to be 3,000 years old. The largest giant sequoia is the General Sherman tree. It can be found in California's Sequoia National Park. It measures over 100 feet (30 meters) wide and 270 feet (82 meters) tall!

Western Wildlife

The Sierra Nevada is home to many animals. One of the biggest is the mountain lion. A male mountain lion can grow to be 8 feet (24 meters) long and 180 pounds (82 kilograms). They are mysterious and rarely seen by humans. Females have two to three cubs at a time. The cubs live with their mothers for up to two years. During that time, their mothers teach them everything they need to know for survival on their own.

mountain lion and cub

Sierra Nevada mountain beaver

Beavers live all over North America. But the Sierra Mountain beaver only lives in and slightly north of the Sierra Nevada. They typically live alone. While they climb trees and swim, they spend most of their time in underground tunnel systems. Mountain beavers are unable to pant or sweat, which is how animals cool themselves. Because of this, they have to live in cool climates and near water.

The mountain yellow-legged frog only lives in the Sierra Nevada region. This small frog has protective coloring for camouflage. If threatened, the frog produces a garlic smell to scare predators away. Its sticky tongue catches insects, but this frog will sometimes even snack on its own tadpoles.

Alaska Range

Which is the highest peak in North America? That would be Denali in the Alaska Range. It is also called Mount McKinley. It towers over most other peaks at 20,310 feet (6,190 meters) in elevation. This mountain attracts climbers who want to challenge themselves to make it to the top. Is this a typical day hike? Definitely not! It is a journey that requires months of training and preparation before making the climb. It takes about three weeks to reach the top of Denali and climb back down.

bald eagle

mountain glacier

The Alaska Range is ever changing. Slabs of rock called **tectonic plates** make up the outer layer of Earth. As they shift and move, the land above them changes, forming new mountains. This is common in Alaska. Cracks in Earth's crust called **faults** surround this mountain range. They have caused many earthquakes.

You would think this kind of **seismic** activity would keep people from visiting. But Alaska and the Alaska Range continue to be at the top of many tourists' must-see lists. Wild animals such as grizzly bears, moose, and wolves roam freely in this area. You might even see a bald eagle. In addition to abundant wildlife, tourists can also see numerous glaciers and even sled dog demonstrations.

A Country of Mountains

There are many mountain ranges in the United States. Each has its own climate, wildlife, and beauty. The Appalachian Mountains get lots of rainfall. They are also covered with trees. Their miles and miles of trails attract hikers from all over.

The Rocky Mountains feel enormous and seem to touch a vast, blue sky. Their many scenic landmarks bring millions of tourists each year.

The Sierra Nevada is a habitat for many animals. It is also a draw for outdoor activities. It is the home of one of the highest peaks in the country. Some of the largest trees in the world are found there, too.

And the Alaska Range boasts a challenging hiking trek to the top of the third-highest peak on the planet. Its numerous glaciers, amazing wildlife, and snow-covered beauty create an environment like no other.

There are many more mountain ranges in the United States. So, what are you waiting for? Head on over to the nearest mountain and start exploring!

Flat Lands

Some people define a mountain as being at least 1,000 feet (305 meters) high. Based on that definition, Delaware, Florida, Rhode Island, Louisiana, and Mississippi do not have any mountains.

Uinta-Wasatch-Cache National Forest, Utah

North Cascades National Park, Washington

Gothics Mountain, Adirondack Mountains, New York

Cascade Canyon, Grand Teton National Park, Wyoming

Map It!

There are many other mountain ranges than the four you read about. There are even small ranges that are part of larger ones. Choose one of the ranges included in this book or another one that you know about. Make a map to share its majestic beauty.

Here are the steps:

1. Select a mountain range.
2. Research the range to learn where it is exactly. Also research to learn its major landmarks, wildlife, recreation activities, and more.
3. Draw a map of the United States. Draw your mountain range where it lies within the country. Be careful to use references and place your mountain range correctly.
4. Label the mountain range.
5. Use symbols to show the things you learned about the mountain range (its landmarks, wildlife, recreation activities, etc.).
6. Make and add a map key for the symbols.

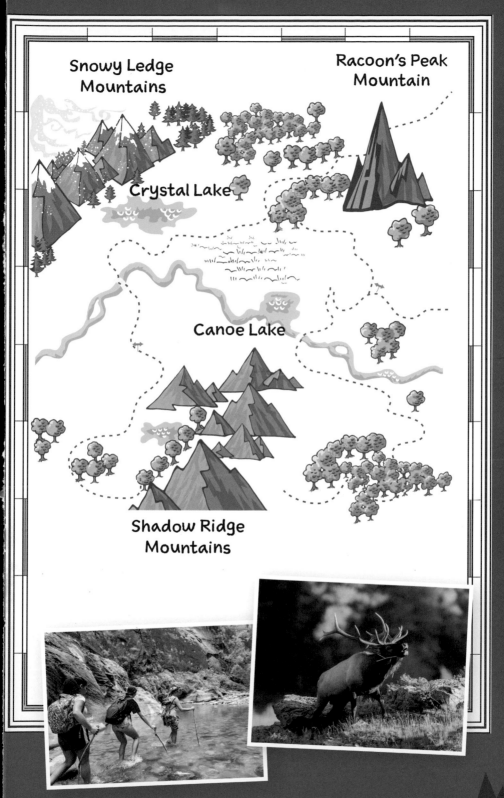

Snowy Ledge
Mountains

Racoon's Peak
Mountain

Crystal Lake

Canoe Lake

Shadow Ridge
Mountains

Glossary

camouflaged—disguised to blend into its surroundings

dams—large walls or barriers to hold back water

deserted—having no people or things in it; empty

distinct—not like others

domestic—able to live alongside humans; tame

elevation—the height of something above ground level

erosion—the process of wearing away

extensive—covering a large area

faults—cracks in Earth's crust along which movement occurs, often in different directions

flock—to gather in a crowd

generates—produces

geological—related to the physical structure of Earth

geyser—a hole in the ground that shoots up hot water and steam

native—born or existing naturally in a particular place

scenic—having beautiful, natural scenery and views

seismic—related to an earthquake

tectonic plates—large, slow-moving pieces of Earth's surface whose movement can sometimes cause events such as earthquakes and tsunamis

terrain—land of a particular kind

turbine—an engine that has parts moved by water

unique—one of a kind

vastness—great in size or amount

venomous—having or producing venom

Denali National Park, Alaska

Index

*This mountain range can be pronounced either ah-puh-LAY-chuhns or ah-puh-LATCH-uhns.

Learn More!

Charles Crenshaw set a record in 1964. He was the first Black American to climb to the top of Denali. A group of 15 climbers braved the long, dangerous trek with him.

Research to learn more about this man and his famous climb. Search for "Charles Crenshaw Denali." Also, search for "Expedition Denali." Use the facts you find to make a booklet or a poster about him.

Think about the following questions as you work:

✳ What was special about what Crenshaw did?

✳ In what ways was the journey dangerous?

✳ What was the purpose of Expedition Denali?

✳ How did the expedition affect other people?

Denali, Alaska